Tales of Light and Darkness

Ahmad Zaidi Naqvi Qureshi

Introduction

The spiritual, supernatural, and metaphysical become ingrained in a reality. Thus, challenging the Reality claimed to be "real" based on a myopic and narrowminded perspective. The doors for various possibilities open that could not be possible before when entering the realm of the Divine Reality and spiritual nature of the cosmos and ultimately in our being.

However, as the Universe is created with a bipolar nature, there exists not only Light, but also Darkness where we find ourselves caught in the schism of the two. At the crossroads of East and West, we must choose a path forward. Do we choose the Good, or the Evil, Truth or Falsehood, or even in some cases doing so willingly or unwillingly? Furthermore, how we bear the consequences of the actuality and its manifestation in our souls.

The concept and role of God is the foundation, and the actual Reality is God Himself.

Part I. From Now till Then

Lusting and not lusting,

Moving and not moving,

Being and not being,

Beginning and no beginning,

Giving and receiving,

Loving and hating,

Worshipping and sinning,

Forgiving and punishing,

Therein lies self and no self.

The Teacher Breathes a spirit of fire,

Into clay of desire,

Both ends burn,

For the Beloved we yearn,

Spaces within space,

Times within time,

Truths in between,

And therein lies the unseen.

Oh Eternal One,

Provide Light in the Darkness

Are we shadows in the Light, or lights in the shadow?

Let us not break Our promises, for You never break your
Promise

In Thee refuge is sought,

Let me not lie anymore,

So We can exist forevermore.

One is Truth and Truth is One,

Love is Truth and Truth is Love,

Love is One and One is Love.

Everything from Nothing,

And Nothing from Everything,

Into and out of existence and the void,

Manifest and Non-manifest,

Immanent and Transcendent.

Oh Light,

Take off the shroud of darkness,

And replace it with the shroud of poverty.

Truly, I am an utterly impoverished beggar before Thee,

For only Thou hast Power and only Thou hast Might.

Oh Great Forgiver,

Embodiment of forgiveness,

Lover of forgiveness,

From Thee we come and to Thee we shall return.

Oh All hearer and All seer,

These voices that whisper,

Damning towards Love,

Reality changes,

Is it You?

Oh Reality,

Deluded by these connections,

Let me not invent a lie!

For it is only Thee I see,

Or is it me,

Or has the Evil One taken hold,

For they cause me grief,

But Thou art the Guide,

In Thee I seek refuge from Thee,

In Thee I seek refuge from Me.

From the Cosmos to Quantum,

From Quantum to Madness,

From Madness to Hellfire,

From Hellfire, Divine.

Oh Most Merciful,

I have displeased Thee more than I have pleased Thee,

And for that, I am sorry.

Infinities within Infinities for Infinity,

Can our finite minds comprehend immeasurability?

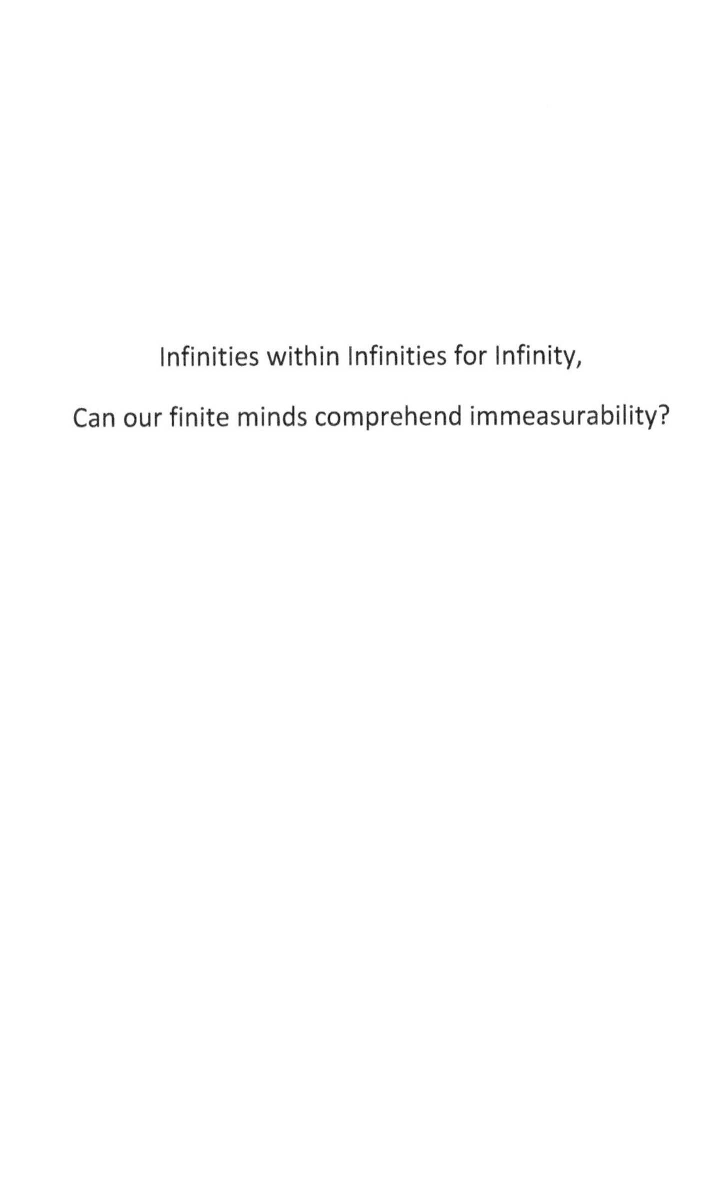

Infinity is Unity,

Unity is Void,

Void is Infinite.

Visions in clear sight,

Illusion and Veils lifted,

Reality emerges,

Can you then see?

Curses and Damnation,

The flames of Hell encompass,

Angry faces and spiteful shouts,

Seeking some relief,

Will there be any?

Oh Magnanimous One,

Let not lies and deceit overcome Us,

Alone down this road,

Continuing for eternity,

Eternity is now.

Confusion and Despair,

The Heart is a Throne,

That can shine a light,

Which you can Trust.

In a dream I saw You,

But You condemned Me,

Remembering Revelations brings salvation,

For in truth, is Truth.

The Ego, the immanent enemy,

From it spews division,

When there is indeed none forever,

In no self, there is True Self.

I am ugly, You are beautiful,

I am poor, You are rich,

I am weak, You are strong,

I seek Thee within and without.

It is gone,

The foreigner named Happiness,

Left without a trace,

On a road leading somewhere.

Get Drowned in the Oceans of Love,

And you will find Hope,

Be Brave!

Let go of your worldly attachments,

These diseases!

Falsify your earthly self!

Eternity Awaits.

She smells so sweet,

She sounds enchanting,

She looks Holy,

She tastes like rivers of wine,

She feels warm,

Oneness manifest!

In Everything The One,

In the Cosmos, The One.

In Power, the One.

In Love, The One.

In the Self, The One.

In the Body, The One.

In every form and no form, The One.

In Infinity and Nothingness, The One.

In all possibilities, The One.

In the Heavens and the Earth, The One.

In Space and no Space, The One.

In Internal and External, The One.

In Manifest and Non-manifest, the One.

In Creation, The One.

In Essence, The One.

In East and West, Yin and Yang, and all Pairs, The One.

In each Particle, The One.

In each Synapse, The One.

In Chaos and Order, The One,

In Quantum and Causal, the One,

In subjective and objective, the One,

In Immanent and Transcendent, The One.

In Time and Timeless, The One.

In all definitions and the undefined, The One.

In the four governing forces, The One.

In the Heart, The One.

In Truth, The One.

At every moment forgiveness is beseeched,

Then at those moments say "thank You",

At those moment, say "I love You".

Rivers of Wine,

Playful dances,

Joyous laughter,

Life Eternal,

A dream not forgotten.

Blessed are the Bringers of Truth!

Blessed are the Confirmers of Truth!

On the Day there will be no intercessor,

May He come! May He come! May He come!

Truly, He is altogether lovely.

Oh All-Mighty One!

You created the universe in a single word,

Power in each atom,

Your might is in Forbearance,

Your might is in Mercy,

Your might is in Forgiveness.

Oh Most Gracious!

In the act of Creation of giving Yourself,

The true and only selflessness,

Altruism is only Thine,

Self-Manifestation!

Let your witnessing and testimony be eternal and forever!

There is nothing else!

Without the timelessness of it, there is only falsehood.

And falsehood leads to Hellfire.

He is Eternal as The One,

He is Eternal by The One.

I am what I believe,

Not what I think.

Please help!

Please forgive!

Please help!

Please forgive!

Please have Mercy!

It is the separation which drowns us in pain,

To Unite is All.

After which there is no more pain.

Your brain is a filter to the External and Internal,

Your beliefs are a filter for your thoughts,

Your manner is a filter for your beliefs,

Your actions are a filter for your manner,

So act!

Lubaik. We stand naked before the Lord,

Seeing deeper into the soul and heart,

Strive completely to shine it so that the reflection is clear!

The core of Sunnah is in Beliefs,

More so than the ritual,

So conform!

There is nothing else!

There is nothing else but Thee in my heart!

There is nothing else.

Testify in this very moment!

For "Verily, Truth overcomes Falsehood".

By the Power of Ali,

And the Light of Hussein,

I put all my faith in Thee and all my trust in Thee.

I seek refuge in Thee from taking away Thy blessings,

I seek refuge in Thee from thy anger and sudden wrath,

I seek refuge in Thee from thy displeasure,

I seek refuge in Thee from Evil,

I seek refuge in Thee from the Devil,

I seek refuge in Thee from falsehood,

I seek refuge in Thee from the self,

I seek refuge in Thee from Thee.

Beware of tricks and lies,

Beware of deceit and conceit,

Avoid the devil's traps with knowledge.

Grant me Criterion,

To know right from wrong,

Just from unjust,

Reality from Illusion,

Truth from Falsehood.

A Dark Magic somewhere in the midst,

Causing delusions and hallucinations,

Or is it Divine theophany?

The magic is strong,

Causing reversals in thought and consequences,

Leading astray.

Infinity unbounded and indivisible,

Continuous and never ending,

A singularity from which comes multiplicity,

All multiplicity embedded in the singularity,

In truth, there is no separating the Void of nothingness and
Infinite and Singular.

Seeking knowledge and hidden truths in all things,

In the Signs, He is.

Creation of relationships that connect all things.

He is also without the Signs and without relationships if He
did not want to see Himself.

"To know yourself is the know your Lord",

The path to self-realization,

Let the heart be a mirror as it holds the essence.

Do you know the powers of the Heart?

That it can transform Reality.

Creating a Reality of its own.

Then on its own it Creates It.

And leaves you bewildered.

What more do you want?

When there is nothing else.

Keep It!

Forever!

And Trust!

Keep reflecting,

For it shows you Grace,

Keep reflecting,

For in it, is gratitude,

Keep reflecting,

And you will find Love.

Don't just believe in One,

Be One!

And honor Him for it.

Blessed by the Saints,

Honor them for it too.

And may He accept it.

Thank You for You!

Praise be to Thee for Thee!

Forgive me for me.

There is nothing like Thee,

There is nothing but Thee.

Enter me in Thy Grace so that Evil in me can be vanquished.

Let your essence in us blossom,

So that we can only see Thee.

Beggars are we before Thee,

Let nothing remain besides Thy Sublimity.

I love You,

I need You,

Please enter my Heart.

There is no reality except the Reality.

There is no truth except the Truth.

There is no essence except the Essence.

I cannot praise Thee as thy deserved to be Praised.

I cannot thank Thee as thy deserved to be Thanked.

I cannot glorify Thee as thy deserved to be Glorified.

Engulfed in Darkness,

Hope is bleak,

Drowned by Tidal Waves,

While sinking deeper,

Behold, the Gates of Mercy open!

Whispers constantly,

Voices is my head damning me,

Lost in a Sea of Chaos.

Leering looks everywhere I turn,

Seem condemning.

A curse, perhaps.

No escape.

The play of Light and Dark,

A never-ending cycle,

Salvation lies outside.

In the Lord of East and West.

Thought broadcasting,

Where those around see your every thought,

Alone, at the center, ridiculed.

The Wall has been torn down and all of you exposed.

I want it not.

I have no choice.

Overcome the tricks of the Ego,

They only lead to ruin.

Remove it from the equation,

And achieve liberation.

Fill your cup with Milk and drink it all,

When it is done, it will be refilled on its own.

Drink it again, there is so much more.

By Him, did he Read the Universe!

Gratitude leads to happiness,

And happiness leads to love.

You give and give and give without stint.

Even without asking you give even more.

As you give you also forgive.

All Praises and thanks are to Thee!

You are in everything,

And everything is in Thee.

For in two, there is still One.

In three, there is still One.

In four, there is still One.

In such a manner, in everything, there is One.

If not Paradise,

Then at least Araaf.

Please place me in the River for cleansing,

Before I meet Thee.

Otherwise I shall stand ashamed.

Your name in every form,

Your name in no form,

Your name in every definition,

Your name in no definition,

Both, Aristotle and Plato!

As Truth, Absolute.

And as Logos, Transformative.

I am the greatest!

I am the lowest of the low.

Signs everywhere and in everything,

This means that, and that means this.

It is illogical but is my Reality.

There is no such thing as coincidence.

With all the possibilities, how can it occur?

It reflects my thoughts.

As does the Lightning!

Man is created in His Image.

A vice-regent.

I see Him in you.

Bow down!

Straying thoughts,

Not condoned,

Please do not hold me accountable.

I love You for him,

I love him for You,

I love You for them,

And I love them for You.

Love for Thee and Thy Messenger is Paradise enough!

Visions flash before closed eyes,

Showing people, places, things.

Meanings extracted, but not known.

Stories of the past, present, and future.

As He is seen, struck with awe of fear.

In fear, trust in Mercy.

With Mercy, comes love.

Miracles before you.

People say "love yourself".

I hate myself.

For it is the self that causes your own destruction.

Did you know there is a difference between the carnal self
and the soul?

Thank You Rabb for letting me feel close to Thee,

By reading Masnavi.

To have faith is to trust,

Whichever dark path you trod on, have faith!

When you witness the singularity,

Complete it with Mustafa!

Behold the Uncarved Block!

From which any form is possible!

From no form to infinite forms!

What is it?

Damnation, cursed, Black Magic, Evil Eye?

Like she said, probably better off dead.

As you witness there is nothing else,

It is Reality more so than your own illusionary existence.

Beware of your Nafs,

Pulling you down to Hellfire!

Carnal as opposed to Divine.

Blessed was he who purified His Oneness,

Destroying all false vanities!

When you say something, say it with conviction.

When you believe in something, challenge it till you are prepared to sacrifice your own existence for it.

The universe is the shadow of His reflection.

"Light upon Light"!

As you love Him,

Know that He loved you first!

Truly You are All-Giving,

Truly You are All-Forgiving.

Your name is spoken in each breath,

For it is the Breath of the Merciful.

Life force penetrating.

Alive and Eternal.

My living is for You,

My dying is for You,

As the veils lifted,

I made a promise to my Friend.

Use caution while on the Path,

For demons will come at you relentlessly,

Causing you to stray for it brings them joy.

By Him, He will allow you to return.

So keep knowledge of Him as your defense.

And never lose trust.

In Your Sacred Name,

My Heart finds Peace.

Are you ready to die?

Have you prepared to meet your Maker?

This disease has killed me.

On my deathbed, let me not lie.

Part II. In the Beginning...many Days ago

To believe is to see,

And in turn, seeing strengthens your faith,

For some, the simplest of understanding is the hardest.

Once you understand the Mercy of GOD,

Only then can you be free.

As dusk approached dawn sunlight creeped up his bed,

His unwonted waking stirred thoughts in his head,

And then that deadly morning, he finally gave in,

With no more tears to shed, there was no reason for him.

The world had left him to be on his own,

Creating such chaos he never would have known,

And betrayal filled him with such faithless belief,

As he took to the river to extinguish his grief.

Torn into a myriad of pieces,

Crossing the point of no return,

Broken at the back,

Time to attack!

Feeling the deadly raven tearing into my head,

Unable to escape its soul piercing beak,

Reaching, screeching, wailing preaching,

Recollecting the old man's teaching.

Struggling toward the shadow of the light,

Running for cover amidst the surrounding fire,

Still I remain a black and white pawn,

Till another day, the battle rages on.

Thinking is good, but realizing is better,

Philosophy is good, but religion is better,

The trees praise GOD who is in the Heavens.

Waking to the sound of blossoming tulips,

Surrounded by the splendor of evolution's glory,

As waterfalls ignite the brilliance of life,

I await to be cradled in the warmth of all that is…Life.

Allowing the Angel to rest her wing on my shoulder,

Uniting two beings into One,

I let my soul travel through unchartered territory,

Still I dream of the Messiah that will complete my never-ending story.

I am everyone,

Everyone is me,

Nothing is peaceful,

You can hear it in a child's plea.

With the myriad of all that is,

Proof of the One!

You tell me, do you see Order or Chaos,

How can the celestial bodies maintain perfect Orbits?

Quantize It if you can!

Left in limbo between lies and deceit,

Is it me who I have to defeat,

Shredded into strips that reveal no order,

Forever lost on the brink for which there is no border,

Yearning the nothingness that will fill my forgotten soul with peace,

The unwanted existence that won't seem to cease,

The horrid disease that infects my brain,

How can I avoid this when it is something I cannot tame,

Seeking the void so that my thoughts stay sealed,

Turning away from the Mercy so that it may stay healed,

Forging my Fears as malicious emotions that burn,

As the Angle of death passes by, I ask Him when will it be my turn.

Into the depths of the unknown abyss,

We tread through the nights of unwanted hunger,

Depleting innocence infesting our souls,

I look into your eyes to find endless black holes.

Restrained emotions left to decay,

Burning desires unleash to find no reply,

Turned away from the roots that hold us,

Following nothing but unyielding lust.

Still you won't understand the burden on my mind,

And still you cannot see the beauty of my Heart,

Gone forever and no path taken,

You will never realize why I feel forsaken.

In bipolarity and the pairs of Creation,

Its essence is and can only be One,

For the other cannot exist otherwise,

They share the same Source,

The difference between Creator and Creation,

So Understand!

There's only One,

And He shares no power,

He holds the Sun,

And the Rain that showers!

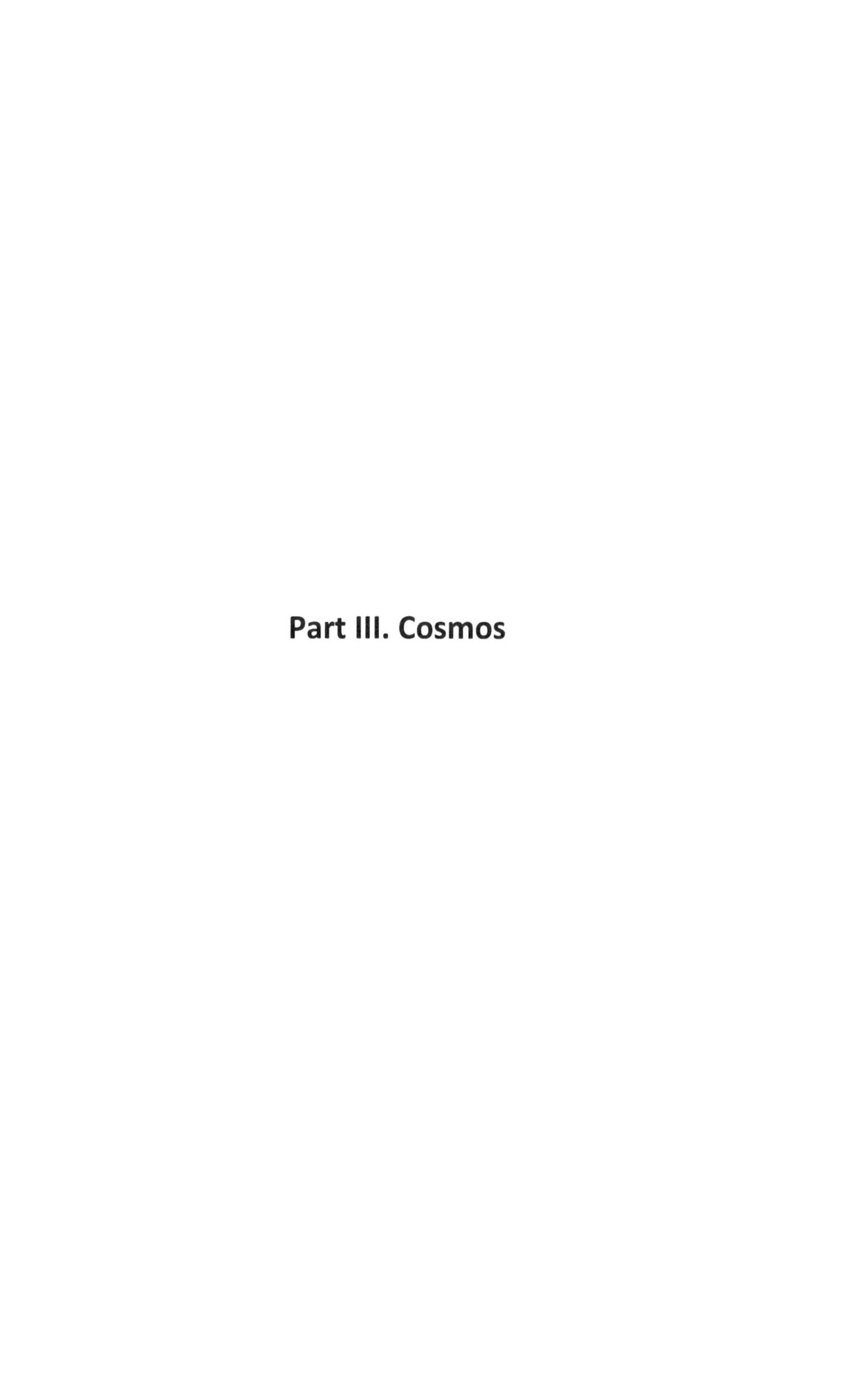

Part III. Cosmos

With the four governing forces,

Unified in the theory of everything,

There is the Unity of Law.

Where there is darkness,

There is also light.

The Line of Truth,

Flawless and perfect,

It is endless if positive and negative Infinity,

Where the juxtaposition is Faith.

Indubitable faith is a conclusion of pure mathematics,

This leads to perfect deductive logic,

Leading to flawless intuition,

Leading to perfect Faith.

Decomposed into each other, acting with this leads to ultimate success.

Believe in the collective and single consciousness of the
Universe,

By affirming your own consciousness, manifested by the
variables of the Universe,

When all variables exist in the a priori singularity,

Is it not conscious and much more?

All phenomena that exists in the Universe,

Was pre-computed before the birth of the Universe.

And in creation, what created it is equal to, or greater than,
it, in complexity.

With the positive, bliss is maintained,

With the negative, positive responds,

Such is a mechanism for Infinite Mercy.

Serving Him,

Also means serving Yourself.

Physical phenomena transform,

But essence is maintained in a new form,

Thus, all phenomena have the same essence,

And allowed to interact in harmony.

Destroy and annihilate Yourself to reach Nothingness,

From which become Everything.

And Thine is the most beautiful Love story

Ameen